D0903095

Animal Classification

Amphibians

by Erica Donner

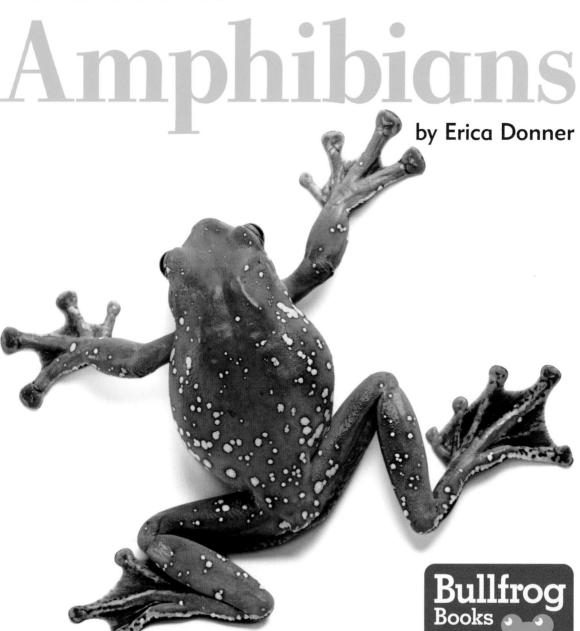

Bullfrog Books

Ideas for Parents and Teachers

Bullfrog Books let children practice reading informational text at the earliest reading levels. Repetition, familiar words, and photo labels support early readers.

Before Reading

- Discuss the cover photo. What does it tell them?
- Look at the picture glossary together. Read and discuss the words.

Read the Book

- "Walk" through the book and look at the photos. Let the child ask questions. Point out the photo labels.
- Read the book to the child, or have him or her read independently.

After Reading

- Prompt the child to think more. Ask: What different kinds of amphibians have you seen before?

Bullfrog Books are published by Jump!
5357 Penn Avenue South
Minneapolis, MN 55419
www.jumplibrary.com

Copyright © 2017 Jump! International copyright reserved in all countries. No part of this book may be reproduced in any form without written permission from the publisher.

Library of Congress Cataloging-in-Publication Data

Names: Donner, Erica, author.
Title: Amphibians / by Erica Donner.
Description: Minneapolis, MN: Jump!, Inc., [2017]
Series: Animal classification | Audience: Ages 5-8.
Audience: K to grade 3. | Includes bibliographical references and index.
Identifiers: LCCN 2016033123 (print)
LCCN 2016040365 (ebook)
ISBN 9781620315361 (hard cover: alk. paper)
ISBN 9781620315903 (pbk.)
ISBN 9781624964794 (e-book)
Subjects: LCSH: Amphibians—Juvenile literature.
Classification: LCC QL644.2 .F745 2017 (print)
LCC QL644.2 (ebook) | DDC 597.8—dc23
LC record available at https://lccn.loc.gov/2016033123

Editor: Kirsten Chang
Book Designer: Molly Ballanger
Photo Researcher: Kirsten Chang

Photo Credits: All photos by Shutterstock except: Alamy, 8–9, 16–17, 20–21, 23tr; Getty, cover, 1; National Geographic Creative, 13; Superstock, 4, 5; Thinkstock, 10–11.

Printed in the United States of America at Corporate Graphics in North Mankato, Minnesota.

MAY 1 7 2017

Table of Contents

Wet and Dry 4

What Makes an Amphibian? 22

Picture Glossary 23

Index 24

To Learn More 24

Wet and Dry

Look! What is that?

A toad!

A toad is an amphibian.

So is a frog.

A salamander. A newt.

salamander

newt

7

Amphibians can
live in water.

They can live on land, too.

eggs

They start life in water.

A frog lays eggs
in a pond.

Look! The eggs hatch.

Tadpoles!

tadpoles

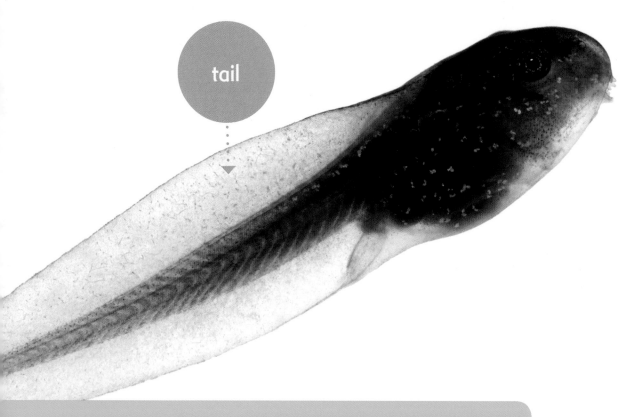

tail

Tadpoles are young frogs.
They have no arms or legs.
They have tails.

They swim.

They have gills.

They can breathe in water.

Soon they grow arms.

They grow legs.

They can hop.

They grow lungs.

They can breathe air.

Now they can
live on land.

Amphibians are cool!

What Makes an Amphibian?

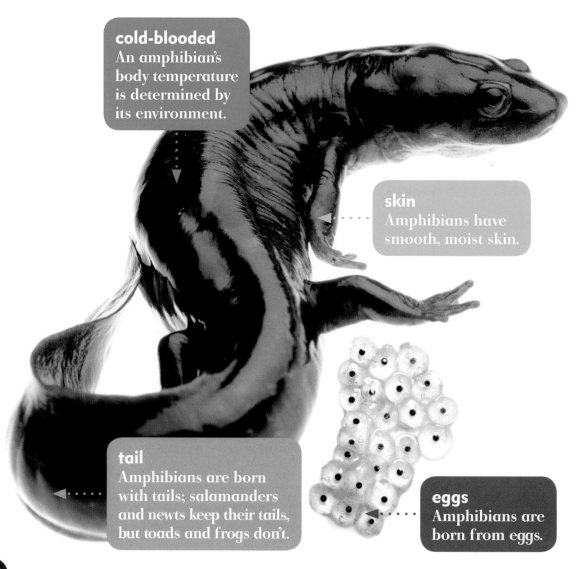

cold-blooded
An amphibian's body temperature is determined by its environment.

skin
Amphibians have smooth, moist skin.

tail
Amphibians are born with tails; salamanders and newts keep their tails, but toads and frogs don't.

eggs
Amphibians are born from eggs.

Picture Glossary

gills
Organs used to get oxygen from water.

newt
A small, lizard-like amphibian that lives mostly in the water.

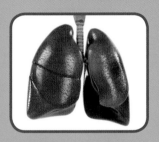

lungs
Organs used to get oxygen from air.

salamander
An amphibian resembling a lizard with smooth, moist skin, legs, and a tail.

Index

arms 14, 16

eggs 13

frog 6, 13, 14

gills 15

land 10, 19

legs 14, 16

lungs 19

newt 7

salamander 7

tadpoles 13, 14

toad 5

water 9, 13, 15

To Learn More

Learning more is as easy as 1, 2, 3.

1) Go to www.factsurfer.com

2) Enter "amphibians" into the search box.

3) Click the "Surf" button to see a list of websites.

With factsurfer.com, finding more information is just a click away.